Full stops

Get started

A **full stop** does exactly what it says. It brings a sentence to a *full stop*. Writing without full stops would be very confusing.

Full stops can even alter the meaning of what you write. Read these sentences and see if you can tell the difference:

> **Eventually Seema arrived home half an hour before her father had to go to work.**

> **Eventually Seema arrived home. Half an hour before her father had to go to work.**

- What happened first?
- Did Seema arrive home before or after her father went to work?
- What is the importance of the full stop?

In the first sentence, Seema arrived home first; in the second, her father left first. If you need to check why, look at the **Still unsure?** note on the right.

Practice

Take a look at these simple examples of the use of full stops:

> **The school bell rang. We all went back to our classes.**

> **I left my English homework till last. It's not my favourite subject.**

> **It snowed heavily on Monday. All the trains were cancelled.**

These are all very short sentences and there are no words to join the first and second halves together – so you need to *separate them with a full stop*.

This section looks at sentences which are **statements**. This means they tell the reader something. Not all sentences are statements and not all end in full stops. Later sections will explain this.

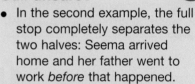

Separating statements

A **full stop** goes between two separate statements. It marks the end of a sentence, and a capital letter marks the beginning of a new sentence.

A sentence is a group of words that makes complete sense on its own. If you are still stuck, *Practise Grammar* deals with sentences in more detail.

Still unsure?

- In the second example, the full stop completely separates the two halves: Seema arrived home and her father went to work *before* that happened.
- In the first example, the two are joined together, telling us that Seema arrived *before* her father left.

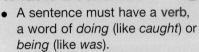
30 July,

What is a sentence?

- A sentence must have a **verb**, a word of *doing* (like *caught*) or *being* (like *was*).
- It also has a **subject**, the person or thing doing (like *Katie*) or being (like *Jamie*).
- Two or more sentences can be joined together into one by words like *when*, *where*, *and*, *but*, *if*, *because* and so on. They become parts of the same sentence.
- So, *when he arrived at the airport* is not a separate sentence, but part of the sentence **Jamie was amazed when** he arrived at the airport.

Remember

If you need to find out more about sentences, *Practise Grammar* will help you.

Try it yourself!

Where's the full stop?

Find the right place for the full stop in the following examples and then write out the pairs of sentences in your exercise book:

> I caught the bus from school to the station I had to walk the last mile home.
>
> The concert was sold out well in advance we had no chance of getting tickets.
>
> Mrs Jackson could not decide between Malta and Cyprus the travel agent recommended Malta.
>
> Jamie was amazed when he arrived at the airport his best friend was on the same flight.
>
> Katie left her books at school she said she couldn't do her homework.

The answers are on **pages 31–32**. Did you get them all right?

If you are not sure, read **What is a sentence?** very carefully.

Where's the full stop?

Here are some simple sentences. At the end of each is a full stop followed by the subject of another sentence. Create a short sentence to finish off each example and write it in your exercise book.

> The flight was delayed again. My father . . .
>
> I have never seen such a boring match. The goalkeepers . . .
>
> My favourite programme is 'EastEnders'. The last episode . . .
>
> We went on holiday to Tenerife. The weather . . .

There are no answers given on **pages 31–32** as there are so many possible correct ones. Are you confident that yours are correct?

Remember:

- Your sentence must start with a capital letter.
- Your sentence should have a verb, e.g. **My father <u>blamed</u> the airline.** or **The weather <u>was</u> wonderful.**
- Your sentence must end with a full stop.

More about full stops

Get started

A full stop goes between two separate statements. The problem is that some sentences are much longer than the ones examined so far. When several statements are joined together, you have to decide when the sentence comes to a *full stop.*

Look at this example:

We overtook an old Morris Minor on the M1. It looked in good condition.

These are two short, separate statements with a full stop between them. What if some linked statements are added to both of them?

When we were driving down to London, we overtook an old Morris Minor on the M1 just before we came to the M25. So far as I could see, it looked in good condition, though it was only crawling along.

All the added bits have been joined on with connecting words like *when* and *though*, and with added **commas** to help the reader take pauses. But nothing has been done to join up the two original sentences, so there is still a full stop between them.

Practice

A sentence should stand and make sense on its own:

The Mayor organised the charity appeal.

There are other ways to write the same information that do not make sense on their own:

- *When the Mayor organised the charity appeal* – *when* is a link to something else which is not there.
- *Organising the charity appeal* – this does not say who is doing it.

So these last two are not sentences and do not need full stops. See if the following examples make this clear:

The Mayor organised the charity appeal. The council supported him.
When the Mayor organised the charity appeal, the council supported him.
Organising the charity appeal, the Mayor relied on the council for support.

Another use for full stops?

Sometimes rules in English change and this is happening with full stops at the moment. A few years ago, the United States of America would have been shortened to U.S.A.; now it is written as USA, without full stops after the initials. This style is now quite correct, but the old form can still be used.

The old rule says that a full stop comes after an initial or a shortened version of a word (an abbreviation). Here are a few examples:

Mr. E. Davis	*Mr.* short for *Mister*; *E.* an initial
Ltd.	short for *Limited*
M.P.	initials for *Member of Parliament*
i.e.	short for two Latin words meaning 'that is' (not 'for example')
G.W.R.	initials of *Great Western Railway*

But beware ...

In the cases above, you can use full stops if you wish or leave them out – but be consistent.

However, there is one common error to avoid.

The spelling *etc.* is short for *et cetera* (meaning 'and the rest'), not a set of initials, so *e.t.c.* is wrong and always has been – unless it stood for *Epsom Theatre Company.*

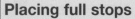

Placing full stops

You might have made sense of the activity **Fit them together** by using a slightly different arrangement of statements. If so, well done! Your version is probably right, too.

There are five statements that make sense on their own:

Mrs Harrison rushed into the room. She was obviously in a hurry. There was no room on the shelf. I could see my book on top of the pile. So I took them off her.

All the other statements support these – they do not make sense on their own. *When the bell rang* and *before she dropped them all* need to be joined to something else.

The last two statements form one sentence, joined together by *so*. Words like *so*, *and*, *or* and *but* join together equal statements. (See the section on **Joining sentences: compounds** in *Practise Grammar*.)

Try it yourself!

Fit them together

Find the activity on **page 15**.

Twelve groups of words are provided, some complete statements, some not. Cut them all out and group them together in ways that make sense. You should end up with four sentences that follow on from each other. When you have done this, copy the sentences out in your exercise book and make absolutely certain that your full stops are in the right place!

Now check the answers on **pages 31–32**.

All correct?

If not, study the note **Placing full stops** on the left.

Where do you put the full stop?

The following examples contain two or more sentences each. There is already a full stop at the end of each one. Copy them into your exercise book and, as you do so, you must decide where else to place full stops to divide each example into two or more sentences. Try to put in other punctuation, like commas.

> **If you turn left into the town centre you pass the cinema the car park is just opposite.**
>
> **Sanjay moved to a new school in September he is enjoying it but he says there is too much homework.**
>
> **Where the river bends there is an old boathouse I will meet you there after you have visited your aunt we can go fishing.**

Now check the answers on **pages 31–32**.

All correct?

If not, try to think which statements make sense on their own. They need to be separated by full stops or joined together by a word like *and*, *but* or *so*. Remember what the note **Placing full stops** on the left says about this.

The last example might read, in its simplest form:

> **There is an old boathouse. I will meet you there. We can go fishing.**

Question marks and exclamation marks

Get started

Are all sentences statements?

Of course not. Sentences can be **questions**, **commands** or **exclamations**.

These often need a different punctuation mark at the end.

Practice

What is a question?

This might seem obvious, but which of the following should end with a **question mark**?

I wonder if the train is running late

Would you mind moving your bags

The first one is asking for an answer as much as the second (perhaps more), but the rule is:

If a sentence is *in the form of a question*, it must end in a question mark.

So the correct punctuation is:

I wonder if the train is running late.

Would you mind moving your bags?

What are commands and exclamations?

- A command is an order.
- An exclamation is something that is expressed loudly or vigorously because of surprise or anger, perhaps. It is often a set phrase like *Good Heavens!*

Any exclamation is followed by an **exclamation mark**. A command might be followed by a full stop or an exclamation mark.

What is the difference between these two sentences?

Close the door, please.

Close that door!

Both are commands. The second is more emphatic and less polite – the exclamation mark expresses that.

Remember the rules:

- Use a question mark at the end of a sentence in question form.
- Use an exclamation mark after an exclamation or at the end of a very emphatic command.

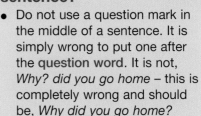

Always at the end of a sentence?

- Do not use a question mark in the middle of a sentence. It is simply wrong to put one after the **question word**. It is not, *Why? did you go home* – this is completely wrong and should be, *Why did you go home?*
- Sometimes exclamations are not full sentences. In this case, put the exclamation mark after the exclamation and follow with a capital letter:

  Oh, no! She's left her mobile on the bus.

- Sometimes, in conversation, a question might not be a complete sentence. *Why?* might be a perfectly correct reply to *I think I'll go home.*

Wait and see

In speech, where does the question mark or exclamation mark go in relation to the speech marks? This can be difficult. See the section **Punctuating speech** on page 25.

Question marks or not?

Remember that a question mark ends a sentence that is in the form of a question.

So what about this example?

Laura asked Craig if he wanted to go to the party.

Is the sentence telling the reader something or asking them something?

It tells the reader that Laura asked Craig; the sentence is a statement, ending in a full stop.

And please, avoid sentences like, Laura asked Craig did he want to go to the party? This is just *wrong*.

How about this?

In the third round, Wrexham were drawn at home to Manchester United. Everybody expected an away win and United attacked throughout the first half. However, in the second half the home team actually took the lead!

Try it yourself!

Which punctuation mark?

Before you try this exercise, read the text under **What is a question?** on **page 7**.

Copy the following sentences into your exercise book, putting a full stop or a question mark at the end of each one:

> Our flight is due to leave at 10 o'clock
>
> When is our flight due to leave
>
> Would you mind passing me the chocolates
>
> I wonder if you would pass me the chocolates
>
> I asked you if you would pass me the chocolates
>
> When does next term begin
>
> I wonder who will take us for English next term

Turn to **pages 31–32** to check your answers.

All correct?

If you made any mistakes, look at them again and remember: if the sentence is in the form of a question, end it with a **question mark**.

What's the difference?

Ordinary sentences can end in exclamation marks if the person writing or speaking wants to be emphatic. For instance, a speaker might be annoyed; a writer might want to suggest surprise. Here are three ordinary sentences. In each case, try to think of a situation where an exclamation mark would be suitable. Write a short paragraph in your exercise book which includes the sentence ending in an exclamation mark.

> In the second half, the home team actually took the lead.
>
> I have no intention of giving him a good report.
>
> Give out the exercise books.

For one possible example, look at the note **How about this?** on the left.

Colons and semicolons

Get started

Do you know the difference between **colons** and **semicolons**?

They look very similar, but have different jobs in a sentence, so you need to make sure that you remember the difference:

- A colon looks like two full stops on top of each other (:).
- A semicolon looks like a full stop above a comma (;).

Practice

The first thing to remember about semicolons is *not to worry*. Punctuation can be perfectly accurate without a semicolon in sight.

So why read on?

Using semicolons can make your work more stylish and give you a useful punctuation mark somewhere between a full stop and a comma:

Full stop

The sense comes to a full stop. Use a capital letter and start again.

Semicolon

The sense comes to a stop. The phrases before and after the semicolon are closely linked in meaning, not by connecting words.

Comma

There is a brief pause. The sense before and after the comma is joined by connecting words.

Examine the following example.

Take these two sentences:

> **Mrs Jackson enjoyed teaching GCSE.**
> **Mrs Robins preferred Key Stage 3.**

There are three ways you can present them:

- Leave them as they are – perfectly correct, but, if you use too many short sentences in your writing, it becomes boring.
- Use a comma – but you will need to add a connecting word, such as *while* at the beginning or *but* in the middle.
- Use a semicolon – the two sentences are so close in meaning they could be two halves of the same sentence: **Mrs Jackson enjoyed teaching GCSE; Mrs Robins preferred Key Stage 3.**

If you have any doubt, play safe and avoid semicolons until you are confident.

And another use ...

Think of semicolons as a halfway option between full stops and commas. This leads to another possible use – in a list.

The section on Commas on page 13 explains that commas are used between the items in a list. But what if the items in the list are long and contain commas themselves?

Read the following example showing another possible use of semicolons:

When I went on holiday, I made sure I took warm clothes because it gets cold in Scotland in the autumn; my compass, maps and guide books in case I had the chance to go hiking; my MP3 player and batteries; my English books, though I didn't really expect to do any schoolwork, and, of course, my mobile phone.

Full stops or semicolons?

It is clear why three of the sentences in Using the semicolon need a comma in the middle. In each case, a connecting word has joined the two statements: *but* and *so* in the middle, *when* at the beginning.

There is more choice in the other four cases. In each case, a full stop would not be wrong, but these are the reasons for the choice made here:

- The first and second coaches are linked together in meaning. So are the two different parts of the view. So a semicolon seems like a good idea.
- There is less direct connection in the other two examples (the evening's activities and rooms are very different things), so full stops seem more suitable.

More on semicolons

The next section is on colons, but the exercises include an activity on colons and semicolons. If you still feel you need more practice on how to use semicolons, wait and see if the activity helps.

Try it yourself!

Using the semicolon

There is a break in the middle of each of the following examples. Decide whether to use a full stop, a comma or a semicolon.

> We all thought the school expedition would be fun but the weather spoiled everything.

> The first coach set off at 9 o'clock the second one waited for the latecomers.

> When we arrived at the hostel the thunder and lightning started.

> The evening's activities were cancelled we found the rooms were very comfortable.

> The building was on top of a hill so we had a good view of the surrounding countryside.

> There was a river valley below us I could just see woodland on the far side.

> We decided to make the best of it this would be home for the next three days.

Compare your answers with those on pages 31–32.

All correct?

If not, read the explanations in **Full stops or semicolons?** on the left.

Create your own

Below are two statements. Copy each one into your exercise book. Then try to think of three other statements to write after each one: the first preceded by a comma, the second by a semicolon and the third by a full stop. The first one is done for you.

> The new sports hall should be finished by September, but the official opening is not until November.

> I am going to see my favourite group next month

Remember:

- You need a joining or connecting word with a comma.
- Following a semicolon, the next statement should be strongly connected in meaning with the one before. In the first example above, it might be about some other building work at the school.

More about colons

Unlike a **semicolon**, a **colon** has a very clear job in the middle of a sentence – or rather, it has three similar jobs:

- A colon can introduce a list in the second part of the sentence.
- A colon can come before a more detailed expansion of the first half.
- A colon can come before an explanation of the first half.

Practice

These examples will make it clearer:

> **We have five different subjects on Monday: Science, English, French, Drama and Art.**

> **It was a real mess in the hall: some windows were broken, the curtains were torn and there was glass all over the place.**

> **It was a real mess in the hall: at the height of the storm, a tree had blown down outside and smashed the windows next to the stage.**

- The first example is straightforward: the colon introduces *a list*.
- The second gives *more details* of the mess in the hall (broken windows, torn curtains, glass).
- The third gives *an explanation* of how the mess was caused (a tree had blown down outside, etc.).

Still not sure?

Think of it this way: if the first half of the sentence leaves you thinking, 'I need to know more', or 'What next?', it is probably a job for the colon, introducing more facts or giving an explanation.

Colons and speech

Some people like to put a colon before direct speech (see the section **Punctuating speech** on **page 25**). This is not really a good idea; a comma is much better.

However, colons can be used for quotations.

Have you ever written about a Shakespeare play and needed to quote a speech? Or written about a poem and quoted some lines?

That is when you can use a colon:

The witches in *Macbeth* say a strange rhyme when they are casting their spells:

> 'Double double, toil and trouble;
> Fire burn and cauldron bubble.'

Some ideas for 'What follows a colon?'

- A list of Jamie's offences (truancy, cheek, chewing in class) is easy enough.
- For added detail, you could put: last week he even got sent off in a school football match.
- For explanation, you could have something like: his mother thought he just liked to be the centre of attention.

For the second example, you could have:

- a list of places
- last year we went to Portugal as well as Disneyworld.
- my father thinks we'd all get bored if we went to the same place again.

There's no dash

Some people like to follow a colon with a dash when introducing a list (:-).

This is a bit old-fashioned so just use the colon on its own.

Try it yourself!

Matching up the statements

Turn to **page 16** and cut out the statements needed for this activity.

Then lay out the statements in the left-hand column, and see how many from the right-hand column will follow on sensibly. Decide whether a colon or a semicolon (or even, perhaps, a full stop) is the best punctuation mark to separate them. Write as many complete sentences in your exercise book as you can. An example is given on **page 16**.

Some sample answers are given on **pages 31–32**.

In the activity above, quite a few statements (from both lists) can be paired with more than one other example. For instance, the statement about shopping at the supermarket can be paired with a list of items or with the statement about going by car. The list of items also fits with collecting for charity.

The important thing is to distinguish between:

Colon   statement + list, or statement + detail, or statement + explanation

Semicolon   two connected statements

So: **The school bus was late again: there were miles of road works.** (explanation)

Or: **The school bus was late again; we all missed school assembly.** (linked statements)

What follows a colon?

Create your own endings to these sentences. You should write three for each sentence in your exercise book: one list, one enlargement (more detail), one explanation:

Jamie found many ways of getting into trouble:

We always like to go to different places on holiday:

Some ideas are given in the note at the top left. Complete your own versions before you look.

Commas

Get started

The **comma** is unusual among punctuation marks because *most people use it far too often*. The first rules to learn about the comma might be:

- Do not use it between two separate statements – that is the job of a full stop or perhaps a semicolon.
- Do not use it to break up a simple statement, question or command.
- Remember that sometimes the use of a comma is a matter of choice.

So what is a comma for?

The simplest explanation is:

A comma indicates a *pause* in writing, not a stop.

Compare it to pausing in speech, for breath, emphasis or to make sense of what is being said.

Practice

A comma has many jobs, all indicating a small difference between the words and phrases on each side of it:

- *Lists* – between the words or phrases in a list
- *Listeners* – after or before the name of the person being spoken to
- *Speech* – between the speaker and the words spoken
- *Clauses and phrases* – to separate different parts of a sentence.

In the next section, **More about commas** on **page 19**, there is a much fuller account of each of these jobs.

For now, learn the first rule of commas:

Commas should reduce confusion. A comma tells the reader to make a little gap between the words or phrases before and after the comma.

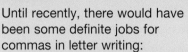

The disappearing comma

Until recently, there would have been some definite jobs for commas in letter writing:
- After the house number and each line of the address
- After *Dear Sir, Dear Aunt Julia, Yours sincerely* or *Yours faithfully*
- Between month and year in the date: *29th February, 1996*

If you look at letters now, you will not usually find commas in these places. It is not wrong to use a comma like this, but it is rather out-of-date.

Don't break up the sense

When the tickets go on sale, there will be crowds of fans at the box office.

In this sentence, the comma is used to separate two statements which have been joined by a connecting word (*when*).

But look at another sentence:

I don't know when the tickets go on sale.

There is no comma here because *when the tickets go on sale* is part of the main sense of the sentence; it forms the direct object. (*Practise Grammar* explains about different parts of a sentence.)

So the rule is: do not break up the sense with a comma.

Helpful hints

The commas game opposite is quite a complicated exercise. Can you work out the right order?

Remember one or two rules that might help:

- Commas are used to separate items in a list – except for the last one following *and*. So, with a phrase like 'a football video and a certificate', this might be the end of a list. If so, the phrase before it must end in a comma.
- Connecting words like *but* follow a mid-sentence comma, so, 'but the team was on a pre-season tour of Portugal' is likely to be the second half of a sentence. Find the first half: without a comma, of course, as that is already there.
- A clause like 'while the school was closed for ordinary lessons' needs a comma before and after (it is not the start of a sentence), so look for suitable phrases beginning and ending with commas.

Right or wrong?

One possible variation from the version given on pages 31–32:

You may have placed the last sentence earlier in the piece. This could also make sense, though at the end is probably the best place for it.

Try it yourself!

The commas game

Turn to the activity on **page 17**.

You will find a list of phrases that, when joined together, make a continuous piece of writing.

Cut out all the words and phrases and then move them around until you have a piece of writing that makes sense. The placing of the commas should help you.

When you are happy with your version, write it out in your exercise book.

Beware: Other punctuation marks are not included; remember to add your own full stops, etc.

Check your version with the one on **pages 31–32**.

All correct?

If not, compare the two versions and try to work out where you went wrong or whether your version makes equally good sense.

Still unsure?

Read the next section for more help.

Activities

Pages 15–18 contain activities based on different sections in the book. You will need to cut up these four pages, so remove them and photocopy them or copy them onto a blank sheet of paper, so that you can do the activities on both sides.

Fit them together (page 6)

Here are twelve groups of words. Cut them all out and group them together in ways that make sense. You should end up with four sentences that follow on from each other. Then copy them out in your exercise book.

when the bell rang

I could see my book on top of the pile

because she never even noticed

Mrs Harrison rushed into the room

from where I was sitting

there was no room on the shelf

she was obviously in a hurry

before she dropped them all

carrying a pile of exercise books

that half the class was missing

where she always puts our books

so I took them off her

Activities

Matching up the statements (page 12)

Cut up and lay out the statements in the left-hand column, and see how many from the right-hand column will follow on sensibly. Then decide whether a colon or a semicolon (or even, perhaps, a full stop) is the best punctuation mark to separate them. Write as many complete sentences in your exercise book as you can.

I found an old coin in the garden	I never practised enough
The school bus was late again	it was over 100 years old
I always worried about my music lesson	food, clothes, household goods and even books
We buy most things at the supermarket	there were miles of road works
The journey took three hours	my friends looked for one, too
I decided to leave the orchestra	it's always such good value
We organised a collection for charity	we all missed school assembly
I tried to find a really good hiding place	we usually go down in the car

Here is an example:

You might think 'there were miles of road works' can follow 'The journey took three hours'. Place them side by side and decide what the connection is. The second part is an explanation of the first – and that means a colon. So in your exercise book you write down:

The journey took three hours: there were miles of road works.

Activities

The commas game (page 14)

Many of the following words and phrases have a comma, either at the beginning or at the end. Cut out the words and phrases and use the commas to help you arrange them into a piece of writing that makes sense. You need to supply your own full stops, but the capital letters at the start of sentences have been included to help you.

- Not surprisingly,
- , over 50 people applying for 20 places
- , but the team was on a pre-season tour of Portugal
- In July last year,
- Mike Stratton,
- hoped some United players would help out
- numbers on the other two
- All those who took part received four hours a day coaching,
- , practical science and various sports
- While the road safety course was also full up,
- the course on football was very popular
- a snack lunch,
- , first aid and practical science
- , presented on the final afternoon
- while the school was closed for ordinary lessons
- , first aid
- , were disappointing
- a football video and a certificate
- The organiser of the course,
- , the council decided to run courses in road safety

Activities

Match the speakers (page 26)

On this page you will find five spoken sentences and five statements of who is speaking. Cut these out and arrange them in suitable pairs. If you wish, you can cut the speech in half and insert the speaker in the middle. Move the sections around and find as many combinations as you can. Finally, when you have decided which are the best matches, copy them out in your exercise book, making sure that your punctuation is correct.

If you don't come in now, your dinner will get cold.

We did this work last term.

We've plenty of time, so let's go to the shops after school.

I'm afraid you can't come in here.

It's all right you saying that, but I'm the one who has to tell him.

Answered the doorman

My father shouted

Jarmila whispered

Ben replied

Chloe said to her friend

More about commas

Get started

Use a comma between the various items in a list, except for the last one with the word *and*: **I entered for the 100 metres, the 200 metres, the high jump and the relay.**

Some points to bear in mind:

- If you have very long items in the list, you might prefer to use a semicolon (see **page 9**).
- In some cases (if, perhaps, the word *and* occurs more than once), you *might* choose to put a comma before the last item: **Bring with you the map, your compass, your coat and gloves, and your packed lunch.**
- Careful use of commas in lists matters. How many boys are here: two, three, four or five? **Mike Leslie Grant Lee and Barry** Only commas can make clear whether there is someone called *Mike Leslie* or *Leslie Grant* or *Grant Lee* or none of these.

Practice

A comma introduces speech. After *He said* or *She whispered*, put a comma before the words spoken. The same thing applies if the phrase comes at the end of the speech and, usually, if it comes in the middle:

'**The trouble with you,' Sally said, 'is that you never pay attention.'**

The sections on speech punctuation (**pages 25–28**) give full details.

Commas also indicate separate phrases or clauses. Here are two separate statements:

The flight was due to take off. We were still at the check-in desk.

When we join separate statements together with a connecting word, we use a comma:

When the flight was due to take off, we were still at the check-in desk.

The flight was due to take off, but we were still at the check-in desk.

You should mark off a separate phrase with commas at the beginning and the end:

The steeply sloping path, going down to the valley floor, was filled with boulders.

or

The steeply sloping path, filled with boulders, went down to the valley floor.

Commas for listeners

If you identify the person or people you are speaking to, separate the name or title from the rest of the sentence with a comma or commas:

Members of the Church Council, it gives me great pleasure to be here.

Now you're here, Joanna, let's listen to your CD.

So what is the difference between the following two sentences?

All contestants in the sprint relay stand over there.

And

All contestants in the sprint relay, stand over there.

The first is a statement, telling what the contestants do.

The second is a command, telling the contestants to take their positions.

Joined with a comma?

As already mentioned, some words join together two equal sentences: *and*, *but*, *so* and *or* are the main ones.

Is a comma needed where the sentences join?

That depends on the connecting word:

but/so   comma

or   no comma

and   usually no comma

I went to the school office, but I couldn't find the register.

I went to the school office and collected the register.

A last word on commas

● Always use common sense.
● Do not over-use commas.
● Always use a comma if the meaning is not clear without one.

Try it yourself!

Where are the commas?

In the piece of writing below, all the punctuation marks are included, except for commas. Copy the piece into your exercise book, writing in commas where they are needed – and, just as important, making sure that you do not include any unnecessary commas.

> When you start a piece of homework it is important to make sure that you have everything you need: books pens paper and if necessary a calculator. You should decide when is the best time to start work. If you have younger brothers and sisters it is a good idea to choose a time when they are out playing visiting friends or doing their own work. You do not want to be interrupted by your sister saying 'Come on Kirsty have a look at this on television.' Your concentration on your work even if you are doing something exciting like English can suffer but you must try not to be distracted.
>
> Finally you have everything you need and the house is really quiet. You open your textbook find the right page check the question you have to answer and make a start. For the next hour except for when you get a drink from the kitchen you are hard at work.

Check the correct version on **pages 31–32**.

All correct?

No? Then try a different way of thinking about commas.

Read the last sentence of the first paragraph again. It is confusing without punctuation.

There are three statements all linked together:

> your concentration on your work can suffer
>
> even if you are doing something exciting like English
>
> but you must try not to be distracted

By using commas you can make them linked-but-separate.

Think of commas as road signs for meaning, showing the reader where to go.

Dashes, hyphens and brackets

Get started

Previous pages have dealt with the main punctuation marks in a sentence:

- *Terminal points* (that is, marks that go at the end of a sentence) which are mostly *full stops*, but include special marks to end *questions* and *exclamations*.
- *Colons* to introduce lists, details and explanations; *semicolons* to act as a gentler full stop.
- *Commas* for all the small pauses, never to separate unconnected statements.

If you are in any doubt about any of these, go back and remind yourself of the relevant section before moving on.

Practice

Like commas, colons and semicolons, a **dash** indicates a break in a sentence. The sort of break a dash marks is generally an informal one, something that breaks up the smooth flow of a sentence. There are three main uses for a dash:

- If a sentence is interrupted, mostly in speech, use a dash: **The receptionist said, 'I don't think Mr Singh will see – ' 'He will when he knows what it's about,' I interrupted.** (If the sentence just peters out, use . . .)
- If you want to put in an informal break, for humour or excitement, use a dash: **Steve saw his big chance, raced onto the loose ball, beat the fullback, cut into the area, set up the shooting chance – and missed the ball completely!**
- The main use for dashes is to mark **parentheses** (the plural of *parenthesis*). When you drop in a part of a sentence without really connecting it to the rest, you can punctuate it with dashes: **It's difficult enough having your friend to stay in the holidays – it's only a small house after all and we have your grandma to think of – without having extra visitors each day.** Note: you can use brackets instead of dashes for this. It is a matter of choice.

What does it look like?

A dash and a hyphen can look the same; ideally a dash should be longer. If you are using a computer, try to find the correct key combination that will give you a dash and, if you are writing by hand, try to make a difference. The uses of dashes and hyphens are, in fact, totally different:

- A dash has various tasks within the sentence, mainly to indicate parenthesis. Also, if you are making informal notes, you might use a dash to indicate breaks.
- A hyphen links together two or more words to form what is called a **compound**: *red-haired, bad-tempered, left-handed*.

More commas

Much of this section deals with the use of parenthesis. This is when an extra, unconnected phrase is inserted in a sentence. Brackets or dashes are often used for this. However, if the parenthesis is short, it can be yet another job for the comma:

The first chapter was so long and difficult, never mind the whole book, that I nearly gave up.

This is a matter of choice. Brackets or dashes would not be wrong.

Work in pairs

Once you open a bracket, remember to close it after the parenthesis, even if it is at the end of a sentence. With a parenthesis, dashes also work in pairs, but never finish a sentence with a dash.

Some suggestions

- The football match could be *close-fought*, *high-scoring*, *heart-stopping*, *nerve-tingling* ...
- The parenthesis could come after *The best holiday I have ever had*. For a short one, with commas, you could try: *not that I've had many*. An extended one might be something like: (*and I'm including that time we visited our cousins in America and toured California*).
- You need Tom interrupting with remarks like *But I'm rubbish at drama*, and then saying such things as *I don't know, Miss, maybe*...
- Try this: We reached the landing which was musty and full of cobwebs. As we looked around, the air seemed to get colder, we heard a strange noise – and the bedroom door swung open.

Try it yourself!

Make your own examples

In this exercise, you need to create your own examples in your exercise book to show the use of hyphens, dashes and brackets. There are, of course, no correct answers to these. Some suggestions are given in the note on the left.

- Use hyphens to link two or three compound adjectives to describe a football match that finished 3–3 with both teams competing fiercely.
- Read the sentence: **The best holiday I have ever had was when we went to Greece for a fortnight**. Now write it out, adding a short parenthesis using commas.
  Now add a longer parenthesis with brackets or dashes.
- Write a brief conversation in play form where Mrs Desai is trying to persuade Tom to be in the school play. Use at least one interruption, indicated by a dash, and at least one sentence which just peters out, indicated by a series of three dots.
- Write two sentences from an exciting story about exploring a mysterious old house. Use a dash to build tension and indicate a scary moment.

How did your examples compare with the ideas given?

Remember that they do not have to be the same.

Still unsure?

You will probably not use dashes and brackets very much in your writing (too many parentheses are not a good idea anyway), but try following this advice:

- If you want to insert a bit extra in a sentence, just a little bit, use commas.
- If you want to insert something in a sentence – and it might cause confusion, because it is so long and there are already so many commas – use dashes or brackets.

Apostrophes

Get started

In the following examples a letter has been left out, sometimes more than one. Where the letter should be, there is an **apostrophe**:

> **The driver didn't see me at the bus stop.**
>
> **Most children enjoy Hallowe'en.**
>
> **We'll be late for school.**

The letter left out in the first sentence is *o*, in the third there are two letters: *wi*. The term 'Hallowe'en' comes from the Eve of All Saints' (All Hallows') Day, Hallow even(ing).

Apostrophes often appear where the word *not* should be. We tend to say *not* quickly, so *do not* becomes *don't*. The apostrophe is used in place of the letter *o*.

Note: There are one or two unusual words to learn: *won't* (for *will not*) and *shan't* (for *shall not*).

Practice

An apostrophe followed by an *s* shows possession or belonging.

Look at the difference between *teachers* and *teacher's*.

The first means 'more than one' (*plural*), the second means 'belonging to one':

> **The teachers held a meeting at lunchtime.**
>
> **My teacher's car broke down on the way to school.**

What if you want to say, 'belonging to more than one'? First of all, put the *s* for plural, then the apostrophe for belonging, but leave out the extra *s*:

> **All the teachers' cars broke down on the way to school!**

What is an apostrophe?

Look carefully at the spelling of apostrophe and check you can write it correctly. It is pronounced 'a-*pos*-tro-phy' and it looks like a comma in the air: my mother's car or I can't find my watch.

An apostrophe has two main uses:
- to show where a letter has been left out
- to show belonging or possession (with the letter *s*).

Whose is it?

To show possession or belonging, start with the 'owner'. This may be one person/thing (*car*) or more than one (*cars*). Add an apostrophe to show possession, then add an *s*.

The car's tyres were flat.

If there are two cars, the apostrophe still comes after the end of the word. But should there be a second *s*? The answer is to use common sense. It would sound silly to say, The cars's tyres were flat, so leave out the second *s*:

Both the cars' tyres were flat.

Problems with the final *s*

Some words end in *s* anyway. When you want to show that a *bus* or your *class* or *James* owns something, do you put an extra *s* after the apostrophe? To some extent, this is up to you:

- What matters here is how you say it.
- If you make an extra *s* sound, write an extra *s*.
- If you say 'That is *Jameses* book', you can write *James's*.

Problems with plurals

Most plurals end in *s*, but there are many exceptions: *children*, *women*, *sheep*, *feet* and so on. In these cases, use the apostrophe followed by *s* in the ordinary way:

children's clothing – not *childrens'* clothing

Try it yourself!

Apostrophes for letters

Copy these sentences into your exercise book, but replace the words in italics with a shortened version using an apostrophe:

> *It has* been very cold today.
>
> If *I am* lucky, *I will* get to the match.
>
> She *did not* call after all.
>
> Claire *will not* change her mind.
>
> *He is* willing to play if Aneeta *cannot*.

Check your answers on **pages 31–32. All correct?**

Remember:

Put the apostrophe where the letters are left out, not between the words.

So:

I didn't make a mistake.	right
I did'nt make a mistake.	wrong

Apostrophes mean belonging

How many of these phrases need an apostrophe before the *s*?

Write the correct versions in your exercise book:

Sarahs mobile phone	five miles to go
cauliflowers for sale	the schools reputation
fish and chips	passengers this way
the groups leader	my friends name

All correct? Then try these more difficult examples. Most involve plurals and possession:

womens rights	Charles Dickens novels
both boats oars	two pounds worth
a girls school	childrens books

Check your answers to all of the above on **pages 31–32.**

If any of your answers were wrong, get more practice by checking the notes on the left.

Punctuating speech

Get started

There is special punctuation for **direct speech**, but not for **indirect** (or **reported**) **speech**. If you are unsure about the difference, read the note on the right, **Indirect or reported speech**.

Direct speech uses the exact words spoken, and there is a way of marking these words separate from the main piece of writing – otherwise the reader might think *I* was the writer, not the speaker.

Practice

Speech marks, quotation marks or inverted commas?

Which term does your teacher use? It does not really matter as they all refer to the same thing.

Do you prefer to use single marks (' ') or double (" ")? Both are correct; in this book we have used single speech marks. Here are some rules for using speech marks:

- Put the speech marks around the actual words spoken: **Lucy said, 'I don't want to go to the party.'**

- If you put *he said* or *she shouted* in the middle of the speech, close the speech marks and open them again: **'If they call for me,' Lucy said, 'say I'm not very well.'** Note where an extra comma has been added: more about that in **More about speech punctuation** on **page 27**.

- If you want to quote somebody else in the middle of a speech, use whichever speech marks you have *not* used so far (double or single): **Lucy explained, 'Nikki said, "We're coming round at about seven."'**

- If you open speech marks, you must close them: look at the last example and see how two sets were closed.

There are two simple rules:

- Be consistent with either double or single speech marks.
- Only use speech marks around the exact words spoken. Do not put them around *she said* or *he muttered* unless somebody (like Lucy above) actually spoke those words.

Are you unsure about using commas, question marks, etc., around speech? The next section deals with this.

Indirect or reported speech

In a story or in a report on a meeting, you may wish to write what somebody said. There are two ways of doing this:

- by writing down the exact words used. This is called direct speech.
- by making it part of your own story or report. You do not use the actual words. Instead you report it:

  Jason said that he had decided to go home.

  This is called indirect (or reported) speech and does not need special punctuation. Do not use any form of speech marks with reported speech.

Speech within speech

The use of double or single speech marks is purely a matter of choice. But always remember: for a speech inside a speech, use the other. So the example opposite could also be:

Lucy explained, "Nikki said, 'We're coming round at about seven.'"

Remember this

You can avoid most mistakes by remembering three rules:
- Put speech marks around the actual words spoken.
- Do not put speech marks round the *he said* part.
- Once opened, speech marks must be closed.

Some suggestions for 'Match the speakers'

There are no *correct* answers, but here are some ideas:

'If you don't come in now,' my father shouted, 'your dinner will get cold.'

Jarmila whispered, 'We did this work last term.'

'We've plenty of time,' Chloe said to her friend, 'so let's go to the shops after school.'

'I'm afraid you can't come in here,' answered the doorman.

'It's all right you saying that,' Ben replied, 'but I'm the one who has to tell him.'

Try it yourself!

Match the speakers

Find this activity on **page 18**.

There are five spoken sentences and five statements of who is speaking, replying, whispering, etc.

Cut the sentences out and arrange them in suitable pairs: speaker and speech. Sometimes you might prefer the speech to come first.

Are there any where you would like to divide the speech in the middle?

If so, cut the speech in two and insert the speaker in the middle.

Write your final versions in your exercise book. Insert speech marks where necesssary.

Place the speech marks

Copy the following sentences into your exercise book and see if you can find the right places to insert speech marks. All the other punctuation is correct and in the right place.

Anthony moaned, Tomorrow I've got to stay in and tidy my bedroom.

It could be worse, replied his sister, you might have had to cut the grass.

They asked me, said Anthony, but I said, You can't be serious!.

His sister told him to be quiet and stop making such a fuss.

Check your answers on **pages 31–32**.

All correct?

The fourth sentence needed no speech marks. Can you remember why? If not, turn back to **page 25** and look at the note on **Indirect or reported speech**.

Did the sentence contain the actual words spoken?

More about speech punctuation

Get started

As well as knowing how to use quotation/speech marks correctly, it is important to understand other punctuation around speech.

Practice

The correct punctuation mark to use between the speaker and the speech is the **comma**:

> Sonya said, 'It's time we went home.'
>
> 'It's time we went home,' Sonya said.
>
> 'If that's the time,' Sonya said, 'it's time we went home.'

Note that the comma is used whether *Sonya said* comes at the beginning, the middle or the end.

But watch out for the exception . . .

If the speaker is mentioned in the middle of the speech and if the first half is a full sentence, then use a full stop before the speech starts again.

This sounds complicated, but just follow these examples:

> 'I've finished with these files,' said the manager. 'You can clear them away now.'
>
> 'I've looked everywhere,' said the manager, 'but I can't find those files.'

If you need more practice, look at the note on **Commas and full stops** on the right.

Which comes first, the question/exclamation mark or the speech marks?

This problem also affects full stops, but it is always more noticeable with question marks and exclamation marks. Some people find it difficult, but the rule is very simple:

If the question or exclamation is part of the speech, put the mark *inside the speech marks*.

So: Faisal asked me, 'Have you brought the right books?'

The new teacher shouted, 'This is disgraceful behaviour!'

But: Did she really say, 'I'm going out with Tony'?

Long speeches

Remember the rule that any speech marks you open must be closed again?

However, there is an exception when you have a really long speech lasting several paragraphs:

- If you do nothing, the reader might forget it is a speech.
- If you close the speech marks, that means the speech is over.
- So, in this case, repeat the speech marks at the start of each paragraph, but do not close them until the speech is over.

Commas and full stops

There has to be a bridge between *she said* or *he shouted* and the actual words spoken. This bridge is a comma.

But look again at the first example opposite about the manager and the files.

The manager speaks two separate sentences: his speech comes to a full stop and then starts again, and in this instance a full stop and a capital letter are used.

More on questions and exclamations

If a speech ends with a question, there are two punctuation marks together: one to show the question, one to show the end of the speech. Which one comes first?

Think it out for yourself.

Imagine the speech is in a play. You might write:

Juliet   Romeo, Romeo,
          wherefore art thou
          Romeo?

The question mark is part of the speech, so it goes inside the speech marks:

Juliet asked Romeo, 'Wherefore art thou Romeo?'

Who spoke?

Sometimes, usually when there are only two people in conversation, you can leave out the references to speakers and just put the words spoken. In that case, just use quotation marks normally – and *remember to take a new line for each speaker.*

Try it yourself!

Split in the middle

Copy the following speeches into your exercise book, but add *I said* to each of them, always placing it in the middle of the speech. Take very great care with your punctuation, not just quotation marks, but placing any commas, full stops, question marks and exclamation marks in the right places:

> When you get back from holiday, come round and see me.
>
> If you're so keen on football, why don't you come to the match tomorrow?
>
> The train was held up at Dunbar. That's why I'm so late.
>
> He's managed to lose his watch again. He's so silly!
>
> I never expected to be back in time, but the road was really clear.

Look at the answers on **pages 31–32.**

All correct?

If not, where was your mistake?
- In the placing of question marks and exclamation marks? Look at the note on the left for more explanation.
- In the use of commas and full stops? Go back to the two notes on **page 27** and read them closely.

Who said that?

Read the following examples and decide who made the final comment about the gymnasium and the classroom block. Then check on **pages 31–32.**

> 'We must take great care that we don't overspend on the new library,' said the Chair of Governors. 'There are many other projects for which we need money and, though the library is important, it wouldn't be right to pour all our funds into it.
>
>   'The gymnasium needs refurbishing and the old classroom block is in a very poor state.'

> 'We must take great care that we don't overspend on the new library,' said the Chair of Governors. 'There are many other projects for which we need money and, though the library is important, it wouldn't be right to pour all our funds into it.'
>
>   'The gymnasium needs refurbishing and the old classroom block is in a very poor state.'

Putting it all together

Get started

Correct punctuation is needed to make sense of written English.

In speech, the speaker can pause or emphasise a word or phrase to help bring out the meaning.

In writing, punctuation marks tell the reader how our words and phrases fit together:

- Punctuation can mark the end of a sentence, a simple statement – **full stop**.
- The sentence may be a question or exclamation – **question mark** or **exclamation mark**.
- If two or more sentences are joined together by connecting words, it is often necessary to mark where they meet – **comma**.
- If two statements are so close in meaning that, even without a connecting word, it seems wrong to start a new sentence – **semicolon**.
- The second part of a sentence may be a list or statement that explains or gives more information about the first half – **colon**.

If a sentence has something separate inserted in it:

- A parenthesis (an extra part not really part of the main sentence) is added – **brackets** or **dashes**.
- The added part may take the form of speech. If the exact words spoken are used, separate them from the main sentence – **speech marks/quotation marks/inverted commas**.

Other jobs for punctuation

This page explains the main uses of punctuation in separating and joining sentences, and indicating the main parts of sentences. Here are some other points to remember:

- A **comma** has all sorts of useful little jobs. It separates words that we might otherwise confuse. So commas are placed between items in a list, when you mention the name of the person you are speaking to, and so on.
- Punctuation can happen inside words. **Hyphens** join words together. **Apostrophes** indicate missing letters or (with *s*) show possession or belonging.
- Though **speech marks** are very important, remember to support them with the correct use of other punctuation around speech.

Practice

Above is a simple summary of the rules of sentence punctuation. However, it is no good just learning them as rules and doing exercises correctly. You need to be able to use punctuation correctly – without having to think about it – in all your writing.

So the final exercise on **page 30** is rather different from the others. It asks you to make the right decisions in a fairly long piece of writing, without any hint of which punctuation mark is being tested.

Supporting punctuation

Here are five ways to support accurate punctuation:

- Do not forget the capital letter at the start of a sentence.
- On the other hand, do not overuse capital letters. Apart from starting sentences, they should only be used for individual names: *Laura*, *Grimsby* and *Arsenal*, but not *girl*, *town* or *team*.
- Remember to use apostrophes in the middle of words only if letters are left out. *It's* means *it is* or *it has*. It is wrong to put an apostrophe in *its* meaning 'belonging to it' (The dog wagged its tail).
- Starting a new line can sometimes make meaning clearer: a new speaker in direct speech, for instance.
- Do not forget to use paragraphs wisely.

Try it yourself!

A final test

What is most important is that you should be able to use all punctuation naturally and correctly in your everyday writing. Below is a story with no punctuation marks. Can you write it out correctly punctuated? You will need to decide where sentences end and where speech takes place.

When we arrived at the station we all felt rather confused the timetable said the London train left from Platform 2 but the departure board said Platform 5 what shall we do said Tony theres no need to worry yet Anne replied the trains not due to leave for ten minutes I decided to see if I could buy a magazine for the journey I wasnt sure if I had time but Anne said the bookstall was just round the corner while I went to get a magazine the others decided to try to find someone to help us the result was that when I came back with my copy of Heat they were nowhere to be seen what a predicament there I was standing in the station entrance with no idea where my friends were or what platform the train went from and now there were only five minutes left I raced towards Platform 5 in a state of panic then just as I caught sight of Anne and Tony an announcement came over the loudspeaker owing to track repairs the 10.45 to London Euston is running late said the announcer and will now depart from Platform 7 at approximately 11.05

Compare your version to the one given on pages 31–32. How did you do?

Sometimes there is more than one correct answer. For example, the only essential exclamation mark is at the end of **What a predicament!**, but there are other possibilities and your version might be slightly different from the one given.

If there is anything you are unsure about, look it up in the section dealing with the relevant punctuation mark used.